STUDENT TEAMING

YOU GOT THIS!

A Teacher's Survival Guide

SARA CROLL

With Deana Senn

LEARNING SCIENCES INTERNATIONAL

1400 Centrepark Blvd., Ste. 1000
West Palm Beach, FL 33401
717.845.6300

email: pub@learningsciences.com
learningsciences.com

Printed in the United States of America

22 21 20 19 18   1 2 3 4 5

Publisher's Cataloging-in-Publication Data
provided by Five Rainbows Cataloging Services

Names: Croll, Sara, author.
Title: Student teaming : you got this! a teacher's survival guide / Sara Croll.
Description: West Palm Beach, FL : Learning Sciences, 2018.
Identifiers: LCCN 2018941749 | ISBN 978-1-943920-51-8 (pbk.)
Subjects: LCSH: Team learning approach in education. | Student-centered
   learning. | Active learning. | Teacher-student relationships. | Education--Aims
   and objectives. | BISAC: EDUCATION / Teaching Methods & Materials
   / General. | EDUCATION / Professional Development. | EDUCATION /
   Learning Styles.
Classification: LCC LB1032 .C76 2018 (print) | DDC 371.36--dc23.

The most important lessons I learned in life came from the bold, witty Irish women who taught me the value of honest, meaningful relationships. They showed me what it meant to be resilient, to have perseverance, and to never hold back from doing or saying what was right. To my mom, Sheryl Croll, my grandmother, Dorothy Peterson, and my great-grandmother, Agnes Bishop: thank you for being a constant example of what it means to be a strong, professional, smart, independent woman. Because of you, I am so much more than I had ever imagined.

Thank you to all the dedicated teachers who welcomed me into their classrooms. Your passion, humility, and willingness to try new teaching strategies to meet the needs of kids is what motivates me. You have the toughest and most important job in the world. Thank you!

—Sara Croll

Acknowledgments

A special thank-you to the following schools for sharing your resources:

Acreage Pines Elementary, Palm Beach County, FL

Calusa Elementary, Palm Beach County, FL

George Washington Carver High School, Muscogee County, GA

Howe Elementary, Des Moines Public Schools, IA

North Caroline High School, Caroline County, MD

Preston Elementary, Caroline County, MD

Learning Sciences International would like to thank the following reviewers: Dr. Paul "Paulie" Gavoni, Erica Eganhouse, Amber Nelson, Heather Ehlschide, and Melissa Smith.

Table of Contents

About the Authors

Sara Croll was an educator in Title 1 schools for ten years. She has taught elementary, middle, and high school and served as a literacy coach where she mentored and supported teachers. She earned her undergraduate degree at Loyola University Chicago, where she focused on service for others through philanthropy work with children locally and internationally. She earned a master's degree in curriculum and instruction from the University of Phoenix and a master's in educational leadership from the American College of Education. She joined Learning Sciences International in 2016 as the assistant to the CEO, working on special projects in the content team. For the past year she has been a part of the research and development team, where she keeps the needs of teachers at the forefront of her work. She focuses on providing teachers with practical applications to see immediate impact in their classrooms. She has presented on topics ranging from teaming to using daily data in professional learning communities to form instructional decisions.

Deana Senn is an award-winning author and the research and development lead for Learning Sciences International, where she creates tools and resources to support instructional strategies such as teaming and standards-based planning. Ms. Senn's educational experience spans the United States and Canada in both rural and urban districts, including the school and regional level. She is the author of several books in the Essentials for Achieving Rigor series, including *Identifying Critical Content, Organizing for Learning*, and *Engaging in Cognitively Complex Tasks.*

Introduction

I was a classroom teacher and instructional coach for ten years. But as much as I loved teaching, I decided I wanted to reach more students and help support more teachers than I could working in a single school. I left the classroom, and for the first time I started working for a private education company.

And what a shock it was!

I was hired as assistant to the CEO with a focus on special projects, a pretty fancy job for an ex-schoolteacher. A big part of my new job would involve meeting the needs of my new boss, whether that meant driving him to the airport or offering my input on projects based on my experience in the classroom. Our corporate office was pristine. There was no code on the copier, and the supply closet was unlocked! I was free to grab supplies without writing a rationale on what I would use those pencils and Post-its for. But I was completely out of my comfort zone. I remember sitting at my desk the first week thinking, *But what do I* do *all day? Who checks on me? Who organizes my time?* I couldn't understand this newfound freedom because I had never experienced it before.

As a teacher, I had been told what to teach, when to teach it, and sometimes even how to teach it. Vocabulary lessons went from 9:00 to 9:15. Lunch was at 11:27 every day, and that didn't mean 11:30. I was so accustomed to the structure and management from school leaders and district calendars that I didn't know how to adapt.

In my former position, when visitors from other schools or the state were on site, I walked classrooms with the school leadership team. But I only answered questions if they were directly asked of me. In the same way that many students never speak in class without raising their hands, I never said anything without the go-ahead from my principal. Then, within my first few weeks at my new corporate job, I participated in a virtual call with expert education author Sue Brookhart, the CEO, and the content team. I really wanted to contribute to the conversation, but I wasn't sure if I was allowed to. At one point, I tentatively asked, "Can I say something?"

"Of course, Sara," my boss said. He sounded slightly annoyed. Had I done something wrong? But after the call, he stopped at my desk. "You know you don't need permission to speak, right?" he said. "We *hired* you to contribute. That's what I expect you to do."

Well, once I knew my expectations—I never shut up!

At first, I was nervous with all this autonomy. But eventually, as I got more comfortable in my new role, I felt valued. I was responsible for myself and my success. When I knew I was completely in charge of my own work, when I truly owned the work, I felt like a different person.

Two years later, I'm a member of the Applied Research Center, where we work in the field with real teachers facing real challenges. Our team works with teachers across the nation to innovate groundbreaking techniques for student teaming, formative assessment, and practical instructional techniques. I support teachers who use daily data in their professional learning communities (PLCs) to inform instructional decisions that make an immediate impact in their classrooms. I am embedded in this work, but I never lose sight of what it was like to be thrown into an unstructured work world unprepared. And I know now that, as teachers and school administrators, the best thing we can do for our students, the most important gift we can give them, is to prepare them to be autonomous, fully accountable problem solvers, people who are adept at collaborating with others, who can think critically and creatively, and who are able to manage their projects efficiently with minimal oversight from supervisors. These are the skills the workforce requires in the twenty-first century.

Meeting with teachers is a constant reminder of the struggle they have with implementing change and developing a sense of autonomy.

Schools often mandate programs and curricula, and teachers may feel they don't have much voice or choice. Teachers struggle with releasing ownership of the learning to students because oftentimes ownership was never released to them.

What does all this have to do with teaming in the classroom? As we will discuss in chapter 1, teaming, when done effectively (and we are going to help you do it effectively), builds exactly the skills students need to succeed in college, life, and the workplace of the future. These skills include the soft social/emotional skills (resilience, empathy, grit, self-confidence, listening, and speaking) as well as the knowledge and critical and creative thinking capacity that employers are desperately seeking.

What Skills Do Employers Look For?

The NACE Center for Career Development conducts annual surveys of US employers to learn what skills they are seeking in new hires. Their *2016 Job Outlook Survey* found that employers are "looking for leaders who can work as part of a team. More than 80 percent of responding employers said they look for evidence of leadership skills on the candidate's resume, and nearly as many seek out indications that the candidate is able to work in a team. Employers also cited written communication skills, problem-solving skills, verbal communication skills, and a strong work ethic as important candidate attributes" (NACE Center, 2016).

What's in It for Teachers?

As we will discuss throughout this book, there are many benefits for students in classroom teaming. But organizing students to work in teams also yields rich rewards for teachers. When I first started teaching, I came home exhausted at the end of every day. Why was I so tired? Why was I losing my voice? I realize now that I was doing *all* the talking. We teachers thought our job was to dispense information and cover content. But when students collaborate and learn from each other, they *own* the learning. This positive interdependence is what makes teams strong and gives students the skills that will put them ahead of the game when they enter the workforce. You will find that you will be doing a lot less of the heavy lifting in student learning as students begin to take on increased responsibility for their own progress toward goals. As you get more comfortable with teaming, you'll also see that you no longer need to *control* the classroom. You'll understand how much you benefit as a teacher from monitoring and listening to student conversations as a way to assess individual student progress. In many instances, when we insert ourselves, we actually interrupt the team's learning. Benefits of teaming for teachers include:

- Reduced need for interventions, or the ability to make interventions more focused
- More time to concentrate on planning rigorous lessons
- Potential reduction in the achievement gap, as struggling learners gain confidence and new skills in a team setting
- Renewed enthusiasm for your mission as a teacher
- Better relationships with students
- Reduction of misbehavior
- Confidence that you've prepared your students for the future

Let's be honest: every year teachers are asked to implement new initiatives. When I was a teacher, the state standards changed on me four times in ten years. But student teaming is *not* a new initiative that will fade away in a few years. It is the way of the future.

How This Book Is Organized

Student Teaming: You Got This! A Teacher's Survival Guide is not meant to be the definitive primer on student teaming. I have included a bit of the research and the rationale for student teaming in chapter 1, but chapters 2 to 5 are meant to be used as you need them, for quick-and-dirty on-the-spot help with student teaming. I hope that as you begin to experiment with organizing students for teaming, you'll keep this book close for reference. You can flip to the chapters or sections you need to resolve issues or answer questions while you're in the middle of a lesson or planning your lessons.

This book is organized into broad categories. Chapter 2, "Challenges for Teachers," covers topics for self-reflection and planning. Chapters 3 to 6 address issues of behavior, academics, motivation, and personality. It's important to note at the outset that these categories are somewhat interconnected, since issues of behavior will certainly impact academics; motivation plays a big role in behavior; personality is impossible to separate from all three categories; and, of course, they all pose challenges for teachers. You'll develop an intuitive feel for how to weight these issues. You can find what you need by flipping to the appropriate sections and perhaps develop your own system to mark issues that tend to come up often.

Within chapters 3 to 6 I offer specific advice under the headings "What do I do if …" For example, "What do I do if I have a student who is defiant?" or, "What do I do if I have a student who is unable to do the work?" Beneath these headings is listed a number of techniques to help resolve or alleviate the issue at hand. Each chapter also contains a desired outcome for the larger category (for example, the desired outcome for behavior of students working in teams) and reflection questions to help you think about and deepen your expertise in implementing student teams.

"Teachers have gone from 'Can kids learn this without me telling them how to do it?' to 'Let's see what they can tell me!' Since starting teaming, I have seen teachers and classrooms completely transform for the better."

—Sarah Sell, Instructional Coach, Grand Island, NE

The most important thing to remember, whether you are fairly new to student teaming in your classrooms or are familiar with this important method for organizing and supporting student learning, is that teaming can occasionally be a messy process. It requires teachers and students alike to cultivate a growth mindset, where risk taking is built into the process of learning, and where failure is a necessary stepping-stone on the way to success—not something to be avoided, but to be embraced. Again and again, teachers who have begun using student teams in their classrooms have told us that teaming is the best teaching decision they ever made. They tell us they would never go back to doing things the old way once they have seen how their students have flourished.

So dive right into teaming with confidence. The next chapter will help you lay the groundwork.

Teacher Self-Assessment Checklist

☑ Do you find yourself fighting frustration, or sometimes losing your temper in the classroom?

☑ Are you worried about losing control if you give your students more autonomy?

☑ Have you tried group work or teamwork but feel as though you need a little help?

☑ Do you leave work exhausted, from not only teaching, but constantly redirecting students?

☑ Do classroom management and/or behavior issues interfere with the learning?

☑ Are some students falling through the cracks while others are excelling?

If you answered yes to any of these questions, this book is for you. You have already taken the first step toward improving teaming in your classroom.

1

The How and Why of Student Teaming

We stand today on the edge of a true international renaissance, unlike anything ever achieved in history. New technologies, higher levels of education, better health care, increasing life expectancy, and the interdependence of our economies are bringing humanity together as never before. At the same time, the ancient curses of humanity—senseless war, environmental despoliation, poverty, and squandered human potential—endure today as ever before. These are problems that today's young people will increasingly face as they grow up. They need to learn how to solve real-world problems around them, whether global or local. Schools must prepare them for such challenges.

—Dennis Shirley and Pak Tee Ng, "Problem Solving in Education: A Global Imperative"

Key Terms for Teaming

Growth Mindset: "In a growth mindset, people believe that their most basic abilities can be developed through dedication and hard work—brains and talent are just the starting point. This view creates a love of learning and a resilience that is essential for great accomplishment." (Dweck, n.d.)

Grouping/Teaming: A group is a number of students who interact while working together. A team is a group of students who share common goals. Members of the team mutually commit to the goals and each other.

Learning Target: The knowledge and skills students must understand and possess in order to demonstrate a lesson-size chunk of a standard. Learning targets provide an accurate guide for what students need to learn on a day-to-day basis.

continued →

Monitoring: The teacher act of checking evidence for desired student learning of critical content during instruction.

Positive Interdependence: Independent accountability to the team. Every team member offers a unique contribution to the common goal. (Johnson & Johnson, 1994)

Productive Struggle: For both student and adult learners to engage in effort, thinking, or learning that is just beyond one's current abilities.

Rigor: Creating an environment in which each student is supported to think independently at high levels of the taxonomy and take ownership of their learning.

Success Criteria: The explanation and details of the learning target; the chunks of learning that a student must master to meet the target.

Team Ownership: Students interact responsibly by sharing their thinking and using evidence to support their thinking; takes conversation deeper after structures of team talk are in place.

Team Talk: Student teams challenge each other's thinking as they work together.

Teacher Verify: The teacher looks at or listens for student evidence of learning and documents progress toward the learning target.

Student Teaming for the Age of Agility

We have entered into a new age, what some policymakers and thought leaders have labeled *the Age of Agility*. This new age has been propelled into being by the warp speed of our technologies, and it requires a new worldview and skill set that most of us have not yet developed. The Age of Agility demands a lot of its workforce: we must be highly flexible, manage uncertainty, solve problems, collaborate, and shift gears quickly—in other words, we must all become very comfortable with rapid, continuous change. As the authors of a report from America Succeeds put it, "each one of us will have to take ownership of a lifetime of learning, a constant process of retraining and reeducating ourselves as the world around us lurches into the uncertain future" (Gaulden & Gottlieb, p. 2).

The ramifications for us as educators are clear: we just can't continue teaching with a model of pedagogy that was developed to meet the demands of the Industrial Revolution. Our old model of teaching—lecture, practice, and review—served us very well when most graduates would go on to secure lifetime employment in factories or in strictly hierarchical corporations. Our grandparents might have worked all their lives for one company, or perhaps two, with a pension to mark their retirement. But according to the Bureau of Labor Statistics, today's workers can expect to change jobs every 4.4 years. "Job hopping is the new normal," *Forbes* tells us (Meister, 2012). Millennials might expect to have fifteen to twenty jobs over the course of their working lives. They can't afford to be static. They need interpersonal and problem-solving skills, and they need to be able to function without the step-by-step direction of a manager or teacher. As long as we continue to organize learning in teacher-centered classrooms that prioritize lessons based on practice and review, we are not helping our students build the skills they need.

"Education is a big challenge now. If we do not change the way we teach, thirty years later we'll be in trouble. Because the way we teach, the things we teach our kids, are the things from the past two hundred years. It is knowledge based, and we cannot teach our kids to compete with machines—they are smarter. We have to teach something unique so that a machine can never catch up with us. Values, believing, independent thinking, teamwork, care for others, these are the soft [skills]. The knowledge may not teach you that. That's why I think we should teach our kids sports, music, painting, art... everything we teach should be different from machines. If the machine can do better, you need to think about it."

—Jack Ma, CEO Alibaba, at the World Economic Forum in Davos, 2018

Which brings us to classroom teaming. Student teaming, when implemented effectively, builds exactly the skills that companies are desperately searching for today, the very skills that foster agility. Teaming allows students to work in settings similar to the real world. Students working in teams practice communication skills and problem solving through collaboration (with minimal support from the teacher). As we will discuss throughout this book, teaming creates accountability for every student in the classroom. It draws quiet students out and encourages listening skills for the extroverts. The overachievers begin to see that they can learn from students who may have different skill sets. The underachievers learn that they have something important to contribute. Teaming helps kids build conflict-resolution skills that they will use throughout their lives.

Nancy Conrad, a teacher and founder of the Conrad Foundation, an organization that combines innovation, education, and entrepreneurship, says that as teachers, "We need to find what lights their candle." Teachers need to put students in settings that enhance the development of critical thinking, analytics, and interpersonal skills. We need students to feel excited about the possibility of becoming mathematicians, scientists, writers, and entrepreneurs, to prepare for jobs that perhaps don't even exist today.

"Faced with the difficulty of putting new standards into successful practice, much less getting kids to mastery, teachers may feel a bit overwhelmed as they search for the best ways to teach students the skills they so desperately need in this changing world. Those skills include the ability to think creatively, deeply, critically, analytically, and imaginatively; to think independently; and to work effectively with others. They demand both analytical (cognitive) and emotional (conative) skills."

—Michael Toth, *Who Moved My Standards?*
Joyful Teaching in an Age of Change

The Teaming Mindset

Students cultivating a team mindset also build *grit*. Grit (n.d.), as defined by Merriam-Webster, is "firmness of mind or spirit, unyielding courage in the face of hardship." *Grit* is synonymous with *resilience*, and resilience is a quality in high demand in the Age of Agility.

But before students can develop grit, they (and we) need to deal with fear of failure. We need to learn to embrace a certain amount of risk, because we can't teach our students to be innovators unless they are comfortable with some degree of risk taking. In our talks with many teachers in classrooms across the country, the teachers tell us that they're afraid to "lose control" in their classrooms. Being in control is comfortable for teachers. Having students sit in orderly rows, raising hands to answer questions and not speaking unless spoken to, is comfortable. But we have to ask ourselves, should our own comfort take priority? Are we prioritizing order and control over student learning and development of crucial character traits?

You may have run across discussions of "growth mindset," and "productive struggle" in your professional learning. *Growth mindset* was a term coined by Carol Dweck and her colleagues as they studied which traits helped students rebound from failure or setbacks and push on. Some of your students will come to you equipped with a growth mindset; others will need a lot of support and practice to embrace this outlook. But establishing the conditions for all students to build a growth mindset is one of the most important foundations for successful teaming.

When your students are working in teams, they will continually be called upon to take risks, to engage in productive struggle, and to recover from mistakes and failures. But why is allowing them to struggle so important? And what do we mean by "productive struggle"?

My biggest surprise, as I've walked schools from Baltimore to Iowa, has been hearing a similar message from first-year teachers and thirty-year veterans alike: they often don't believe students are up to the many challenges of teaming. It's not that these teachers don't have high expectations, or that they don't truly believe in their students; they simply don't think the kids in their classrooms can self-manage or grapple with problems without adult expertise. But as we work together on teaming, they soon realize that, although they are needed as resources and experts to clear up misconceptions and verify what students have learned, they should refrain from setting themselves up as gatekeepers of knowledge. Jonai Senior, a teacher at Carver High School in Muscogee County, Georgia, told me that for her, the struggle can be hard to watch. As teachers, we naturally want to step in and save students when they seem to be floundering. It is our instinct to swoop in and offer our expertise. But more important than instilling knowledge, she found, is "letting the beautiful struggle happen."

In classroom after classroom, teachers find that students can do the work if you let them! Once they are given permission, students love problem solving. Kids know how to use technology so much better than their parents and grandparents because they are intuitive, curious, fearless, and proactive. They naturally have these qualities. They don't always, however, have the skills necessary to work together in teams effectively.

Teaming requires a deliberate, focused approach with clear norms, protocols, and roles (examples of these are provided throughout the book and in the appendix). The hope, however, is that as students grasp these concepts, they soon become fluid when implementing them. The teacher no longer needs to prompt with scripted question stems or talking gems. As students advance in their teaming practice, they learn to politely disagree, revise their thinking, and come to conclusions based on evidence rather than emotions.

When you see this transformation in your own classroom, you'll know that all the late nights grading papers, attending meetings, and planning for state requirements and other mandates are worth it. You are literally shaping the minds of the future. Pretty impressive!

What Is Productive Struggle?

"The idea of productive struggle arose from the Trends in International Mathematical and Science Study (TIMMS) and was investigated by Stigler, Gallimore, and Hiebert (2000) in their comparison of global teaching practices. Hiebert and Wearne (2003) and Hiebert and Grouws (2007), among others, went on to define and identify the benefits of productive struggle in fostering resilience, perseverance, engagement in learning, and achievement. The term has since entered the mainstream of educational language and thought. Productive struggle, for both students and adult learners, means to engage in effort, thinking, or learning that is just beyond one's current abilities; the concept is similar to K. Anders Ericsson's (2003) definition of *deliberate practice*. Studies have found that students engaged in productive struggle in math, for example, retain the material better, evidence higher levels of conceptual thinking, and are able to offer more alternative ways to solve problems (Kapur, 2016)."

—From *The Gritty Truth of School Transformation*, by Amy Dujon

The Teacher's Role

As a teacher implementing student teams, your role is to set the foundation for successful teaming. As we note in this book, it's best to start small if you're just beginning to get familiar with student teaming. Pick a subject or time of day to lay the groundwork. Below are eleven steps to get you started or refresh your teaming procedures for a new year.

1. Build a classroom culture in which students feel comfortable making mistakes. Here are some ideas:

   ‣ Cover the walls with motivational and inspirational posters about growth mindset, grit, and academics.

   ‣ Showcase students' interests and successes (multiplication club, good citizenship, effort, character building, academics).

   ‣ Welcome students at the door and include them in conversations.

   ‣ Give students as many opportunities for voice and choice as you can: you are building autonomy and grit.

2. Introduce the idea of teaming to your class. Give them the big picture: how teams will help them build the skills they

need to succeed. If possible, show them some model video examples of students working in teams.

3. Brainstorm with students to come up with three to five essential norms for team behavior. Keep norms positive ("Be respectful" rather than "Do not disrespect").

What does a good team

 Look like?

- Working cooperatively (sharing supplies)
- Following directions (on task)
- Smiling
- Taking turns

Sound like?

- On topic
- Respectful conversation (using kind words)
- Being polite (please, thank you)
- Good listeners

Figure 1.1: What does a good team look like and sound like?

4. Agree as a class on these norms and post them prominently.

5. Practice and model the norms. Role-play. Show nonexamples.

6. Put students in teams of four. Ask students to create a name or use friendly competition to inspire team pride and break the ice.

7. Introduce roles and expectations for each team. Post roles and question stems prominently (see appendix for examples of question stems and roles).

8. Gather team facilitators for a quick group huddle to ensure that they understand their roles.

9. Give teams an introductory task to begin teamwork. This task

may be simple and less rigorous while they are practicing. You will build to rigorous team projects over time.

10. Walk around and monitor your teams. Observe student conversations. Let them struggle productively with academics, personality issues, or behavior before you step in.

11. Use the chapters in this book to address any issues that arise.

See appendix for more examples of inspirational and motivational posters.

Effective Teaming Requires Clear Roles and Expectations

A TEAM IS MUCH MORE THAN A GROUP

"When students are working in teams, they learn social skills. I used to have quiet students who would just agree with everyone in a group. But now, as a team, they have roles and they have to talk to each other and be accountable."

—Laura Royer, fifth-grade teacher, Preston, MD

As a teacher, you've probably worked with student groups at one time or another—or perhaps even participated in group projects as a student yourself. But student groups are often unsuccessful because learning targets, a clear focus, success criteria, and protocols are not in place (students routinely complain, for example, that one or two students "do all the work").

But effective student *teaming* is not the same thing as *group work*. Student teams have clear protocols and procedures, like the ones pictured above, that are designed to help students learn and communicate effectively. Teams have roles (a team facilitator and a team learning monitor, for example). They also share clear expectations for the work outcomes that are accessible to all the members. In this model of student teaming, standards-based learning targets and success criteria are carefully spelled out, and students track their own progress to the learning targets. Because roles and protocols are in place, there is little opportunity for some students to coast while others overperform. In short, student teams behave like *teams*. The success of the team is success for all. Or, as fifth-grade teacher J. D. Faxon put it: "Teamwork, A Simple Definition: less ME, more WE. Teaming sets students up for the real-world problems we face every day with coworkers, families, and friends."

SETTING AND REINFORCING NORMS AND EXPECTATIONS

Implementing teams effectively requires that we make team norms and expectations for behavior clear and immediate. Students will need regular reminders and redirections, sometimes on the spot, as they practice new behaviors and begin to form new habits. As teachers, we need to form new habits, too. We need to get in the habit of regularly, and immediately, reminding students when they are straying from established norms and procedures.

For example, in one school I observed a teacher walking her students back from lunch. The hallway rules were "No talking while walking back to our room, keep shirts tucked in, keep hands to yourselves." But some students were quietly whispering to each other, one kid had a hanging shirttail, and two others were playing around. When the class returned to the room, the teacher announced who had lost recess due to talking in the hallways, who had shirts untucked, and who hadn't kept hands to themselves.

Perhaps rightly, the students complained. "You were right there, why didn't you say anything? We didn't know!" The truth is, some students might have known the rules of the hallway. Some may have forgotten, temporarily. Others may have missed one rule entirely. However, if the teacher had reiterated the rules and expectations *before* setting off for her walk with her students, and during the walk, if necessary, it would have saved some grief.

Students should never have to guess what to do when it comes to norms and expectations. Yes, we should allow students to struggle with problem solving and critical thinking around academic tasks and projects. But expectations for appropriate behavior and the success criteria for meeting learning targets should be crystal clear. There is no reason to send students on a treasure hunt to figure out what they need to do to meet a learning target. They should be clear about the intention of the lesson. They should know how to behave respectfully to team members. We need to tell them, retell them, and post our expectations and norms on the classroom walls—and gently guide them back when they stray.

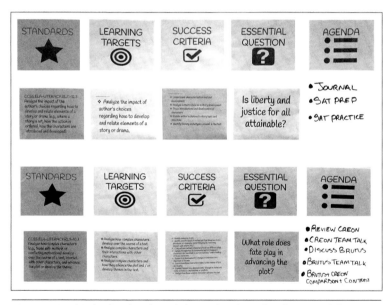

Figure 1.2: This high school English teacher has clearly posted the lesson expectations.

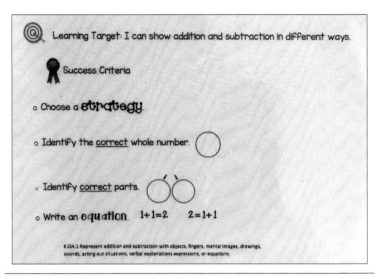

Figure 1.3: This kindergarten teacher uses clear success criteria as a support for students as they work in teams.

In teaming, we also need to define our expectations for how students continue to develop their interpersonal skills. Claude Charron, principal of a private high school in Miami, notes how important it is to teach and reinforce the so-called soft skills like respect and active listening when students work in teams. "Students solving real-world problems and working in teams with a common goal makes all the difference. We focus so much on the documentation and the evidence of learning, but we can't expect that students just naturally know how to interact appropriately within a team."

I know you're probably thinking, *Ha! I know some adults who need these skills.* Just think of the impact it would have if you started building these skills with students as young as five years old!

Teaming Builds Social-Emotional Learning Skills

"Transforming a school for rigorous instruction and implementing systems for rigorous learning require a thorough understanding and acknowledgment of the importance of social-emotional learning (SEL). Zins, Bloodworth, Weissberg, and Walberg have defined SEL as 'the process through which children enhance their ability to integrate thinking, feeling, and behaving to achieve important life tasks' (2007, p. 194). Further, the Collaborative for Academic, Social, and Emotional Learning (CASEL, 2003) identifies five core skill areas associated with SEL: self-awareness, social awareness, self-management, relationship skills, and responsible decision-making. Studies have shown that these skills correlate with improved academic performance (Wang, Haertel, and Walberg, 1997).

"For students who work in teams, social-emotional skills are critical to successful learning. Students working autonomously in teams must regulate their own behavior and the behavior of peers. They must develop social awareness and relationship skills, such as conflict resolution and empathy, in order to provide feedback and coach each other. A truly collaborative learning community will only function to the level that the members have practiced and mastered SEL skills."

—Amy Dujon, *The Gritty Truth of School Transformation*

2

Challenges for Teachers

It's like a trust thing. I had to build a trust that my students could do it, and they had to build a trust in each other. Once the trust was there, through structure, teaming [became] a powerful tool to use in the classroom.

—Nikki Janulewicz, fourth-grade teacher, Grand Island, NE

It's the struggle of letting go, but then you see the growth of your student, and their thriving attitudes, and you realize life is good. Let your students drive their learning.

—Keo Leiser, ELL teacher (K–5), Grand Island, NE

Are they getting it right? Are they learning it the right way? I want to micromanage it more ... that's the struggle, I guess.

—Angie Whitsett, fifth-grade teacher, Grand Island, NE

Overview

Teaming requires building trust with students, letting go of control, and being prepared for the unexpected. We know we're responsible for our students' success. We have students at various levels of ability in our classrooms, and we want to make sure each one is getting the right instruction. We're under intense pressure to close the achievement gap. We want to fix errors and misconceptions immediately. All these pressures make us want to step in, to solve problems for our students, even to micromanage our students' learning. And that's a tough habit to break.

At the same time, our classes are often quite large, and the sheer number of students makes it difficult to verify learning for every student every day. We worry that the class might spin out of control, that kids might veer off topic, that behavior issues could blow up. All these issues make implementing teamwork a scary prospect for many of us.

To be blunt: when students work in teams, the teacher is no longer in control. Paradoxically, that's the very reason we *want* students to work in teams. Teaming requires students to build autonomy, resilience, self-confidence, and communication skills; to create strategies for conflict resolution; to develop empathy; and to work on monitoring and modifying their own and others' behavior. Still, for many of us, releasing authority and control to students will be an enormous challenge. Like the teachers we quote in this chapter, we must learn to *trust* ourselves and our students.

An Instructional Coach Reflects on Getting Started with Teaming

At the onset of learning about teaming, it's common to hear, "My students can't talk with one another without fighting." This is very possibly true. Students may need to be taught how to talk with one another productively. This can be modeled with a coach and the teacher, or students. Students need to be clear on what productive teams look like (where they're going to sit, and what it should/could sound like). Although this may seem forced at first, with some practice, the language will be heard throughout the building. Practice, practice, practice. If students aren't discussing like you've hoped, don't assume they know how.

Teachers work so hard to plan amazing tasks, so it can be frustrating when things don't go as planned. Reflect: what exactly didn't go well? Was the minilesson too long? Were there too many directions? Were they ready for this task? Don't get bent out of shape because something didn't work, think about why and make an adjustment. Teachers have so much on their minds to fit into a task before they start the lesson, but if the *teacher* is struggling to fit it all in, think about how the *students* feel.

Teachers new to teaming are often overwhelmed on how to get started. I've seen many teachers have success by using a nonrigorous task to allow students to feel successful. Starting with nonrigorous tasks helps students begin to be more reflective on the purpose of teaming. I've seen some classrooms, for example, use a simple puzzle, each member with their own pieces to build teaming skills. It's important to allow a little (not a lot!) of time for students to understand why they're teaming and how it's beneficial to complete a task in a team, and get feedback from a teammate. Students can learn so much from one another. I've seen students go from being uncomfortable with speaking in a group to speaking in front of the class. I'm confident that this new confidence was a result of teaming.

The benefits are intense. The tasks are tricky, especially when you're deciding if the task is built for a team or an individual. The tasks you choose should require a team to complete. Teams can complete high-taxonomy tasks that teachers would have never expected. Discussions and disagreements used in teaming build skills needed at any age. It's so important for students to know how to talk through disagreements, and elaborate on agreements. In most any job, we are required to work with others. It's absolutely vital that we start getting our students ready for their future.

—Erica Eganhouse, instructional coach, K–5 title support, building technology specialist, Howe Elementary, Des Moines, IA

Techniques for Addressing Challenges for Teachers

BUILDING TRUST

What do I do if I don't trust that my kids can work in groups?

Try these techniques:

- Begin with small steps. You may want to try pairing students before putting them in teams to help them begin to build respectful communication skills, for example.

- Pulling a small team together and having the members work at a reading table, with the teacher sitting in as a facilitator, could be a start.

- You don't need to use teaming for every subject every day. Try teaming for one subject or unit, or part of a unit.

- Pick one or two days a week to implement teaming

- Practice, model, and remember that you will continue to reinforce procedures and soft skills throughout the year.

ISSUES OF CONTROL

What do I do if I lose control of the classroom?

Be clear about what you mean by "losing control." A noisy, messy classroom is not necessarily "out of control," though it may be more energetic than you're used to. A noisy environment where kids are learning may be closer to "organized chaos" than just chaos.

Try these techniques:

- Walk from team to team and listen to conversations. Are students off task? Or are they doing the work?

- Be sure to verify the learning. Don't assume students are working or that they understand the content.

- Make sure that you have deliberately planned for teaming.

Are your anchor charts, posters, structures, and norms fully in place?

- If the class really is not engaged in learning, stop, have students return to their individual desks, and review norms.

- Pull all the facilitators or quality checkers to review norms while other students continue work.

- Reflect on the planned lesson. Did you set your students up for teaming success?

Avoiding the "Island"

Traditionally, when teachers start out with group work, they will remove "problem" or defiant students, thinking they will avoid a breakdown in the learning. As I have walked schools, I frequently notice the "island." This is a student removed from the team structure and isolated at their own desk.

For example, one student, Marcus, was always on his own island. He was often described as a behavior problem by teachers. He was playful and distracted others, so he was removed from the group. During direct instruction, the teacher often told students to "turn and talk to your neighbor about ..." or "discuss in your teams ..." Marcus did not have a team or a neighbor to talk to.

As teachers, we have all had a Marcus in our classrooms. We react because we know we need to keep the learning going and we can't allow one student to interrupt instruction. However, removing Marcus from the team was not helping him. He was now isolated and unable to do the work with the same resources as his classmates. Not only was he singled out physically, it also affected his attitude. He felt frustrated. But instead of telling his teacher why, he just continued to act out. The other students saw him as a troublemaker. If there was a chance that he could earn his place back on a team, the students would groan and complain about having to work with him. They did this right in front of him. How could anyone deal with that level of direct criticism?

The point is, if learning is at a complete stop due to one student, there are strategies that can help redirect the student and get them back with their team. We shouldn't use teams as an award that is earned, but rather as the expectation for all students. Working together with different skill levels, personalities, and possible behavior problems are exactly the soft skills that the team will need to build. If we equip students with the strategies discussed in this book, teachers will no longer need to abandon students to their own island.

What do I do if I find myself stepping in when I should be releasing?

Try these techniques:

- Keep your hands behind your back or in your pockets as a reminder to hold back.

- Use a tracking device or a tablet to keep track of student learning.

- Wear a wristband, and snap it to remind yourself not to "oversupport." (Don't get carried away and hurt yourself!)

- Keep sticky notes or anecdotal notes in a notebook to verify student learning.

- Anchor charts and desk reminders are not just for students. They can help you remember not to step in when it's not required.

- Ask yourself at the end of each lesson: Who did most of the talking today? Who did most of the work today?

- Keep reminders on your desk or in a notebook.

- Post visual cues in a prominent place as a reminder while you are teaching.

ADDRESSING ISSUES ON THE SPOT

What do I do if I thought I had a great lesson plan, and it's not working?

Ever found yourself teaching a class, only to be met with blank stares? This may be the *perfect* time to incorporate teams. We teachers don't always use language kids can hear—often peers can explain concepts in ways that are a lot more kid-friendly.

- Try letting student peers work through their understanding of concepts or problems. Teachers need to introduce new concepts via whole class instruction, but once that's done, get students teaming to practice and deepen new knowledge.

- If the teaming isn't working, think about whether you tried to incorporate teams too soon. It's okay to stop teaming and pull back to whole group instruction: teaming may not be for every subject every day.

What do I do if I need to rearrange teams on the fly?

Occasionally you'll need to mix up your teams. As we noted in other chapters, there may be behavior issues, self-esteem issues, or academic issues that can be addressed by a quick reshuffle.

Try these techniques:

- Use a randomizer app to randomize teams.
- Have kids draw popsicle sticks.
- Pair up teams by birthday.
- Strategize in advance for mixed-ability groups.
- Have facilitators stand up and rotate to different teams to change group dynamics.

What do I do if we run out of time?

In their enthusiasm, kids can stray off task and run out of time.

Try these techniques:

- Set a timer. When teams are introduced, give them a specified time frame to introduce themselves and discuss their roles.
- Remind kids of time chunks (thirty minutes, fifteen minutes, five minutes, two minutes).
- Teach kids to use sticky notes in a "parking lot" for ideas they don't have time to get to.
- Assign a group timekeeper role.

PLANNING FOR TEAMING

How do I utilize PLC or planning time to generate strategies for teaming?

Remember, you don't have to go it alone. You have creative ideas, and you can be sure your peers do too. They may have strategies for teaming that you haven't thought of.

Try these techniques:

- Use time during planning periods to visit other teachers and see what they are doing.

- Share success stories and struggles in your PLCs. What worked? What didn't work, and why?

- Make an effort to share and collaborate with your colleagues. The people you talk to every day at work may be underutilized resources.

MEETING STUDENTS WHERE THEY ARE

Students will go to the next grade level taking the teaming skills they have learned with them. Gradually, during the course of the year, their conversations will become more fluid and authentic without the use of anchor charts, question stems, or additional supports. Students will use the conflict-resolution skills they learn in your classroom not only in the classroom setting, but in life. These are the skills that will prepare them for the future.

Next year, although *you* may have advanced in your learning, be ready to meet your new students where they are. Your incoming students probably need to start from square one. Don't forget the baby steps. New students will have to struggle with content, with protocols, with personality, just as your previous classes did. Remember that productive struggle is a critical part of the process. Many students won't have gained the skills from previous classes, or from personal experience, to handle academic struggle or personality conflict yet, so be patient and begin slowly.

Desired Outcomes for Teachers Implementing Teaming Strategies

The first desired outcome is that you will eventually implement teaming as a part of your daily instruction. Additionally, students will be better prepared for school, life, and the workforce. They will have positive interdependence and work with a variety of people. And they will become accountable for their own learning. Finally, you and your students will have fun and grow.

REFLECTION QUESTIONS

- What challenges can I foresee to better equip myself for teaming? How can I be ready for the unexpected? For the everyday challenges of teaming with kids?

- What habits, go-to methods, or unconscious "teaching script" may I need to shift or let go of in order to let this learning occur? What preconceptions do I have about "good teaching" that I may need to revise in order to be successful?

- Am I saving students unnecessarily? How can I help them help themselves?

FURTHER READING

The Gritty Truth of School Transformation: Eight Phases of Growth to Instructional Rigor by Amy Dujon

Who Moved My Standards? Joyful Teaching in an Age of Change by Michael Toth

The Inner World of Teaching by Robert and Jana Marzano

Radical Candor by Kim Scott

3

Addressing Issues of Behavior

Working in teams is both beneficial to student metacognitive processes and building social relationships for students with emotional behavioral disorders. Student learning is enhanced through cooperative discourse strategies that allow them to participate in multimodal ways.

—Sarah Courtemanche, middle school special
education teacher, Pawtucket, RI

Overview

When we're planning team-centered lessons, we want to be sure we have put clear procedures in place so students understand our expectations and what norms of behavior are acceptable in our classrooms. We are going to introduce students to teaming norms and routines with the expectation that they will respect those norms and adhere to those routines. Easier said than done. In this chapter we look at techniques for dealing with defiance, addressing dependence, helping students follow routines, and managing high-energy students.

As we implement team structures, we need to grant students a good deal of autonomy and independence—maybe much more than we're used to! Wherever possible, we want our expectations to mirror real life. Students ought to be able to, for example, sharpen their pencils, go to the restroom, find supplies, and collaborate with their team and other teams seamlessly, without interrupting the lesson or the work of their peers. Students don't have to ask the teacher for everything. They are able to make their own decisions. When we give students this freedom with structures and parameters, they don't abuse their freedom because they don't feel as though they are getting away with something. They are simply acting as mature mini-adults. We must operate as if the classroom belongs not just to us, but to our students. They are full members of the classroom culture and community.

And similarly, *we* need to refrain from interrupting the learning. Students should be treated respectfully, and issues of behavior addressed quietly without disrupting the entire team or the whole class. How many times have we seen teachers bring a lesson to a screeching halt just to address a single student's behavior? The student obtains the teacher's attention and usually gets others off task due to the disruption. The entire focal point becomes the student's misbehavior and the teacher's reaction. We may need to retrain ourselves to step back when we can to keep the flow.

For example, recently at a local elementary school, I observed two very different classrooms. Classroom A was a traditional, teacher-centered classroom, where tables of students were working on math worksheets. Just down the hall, Classroom B was implementing teaming structures. Both classrooms were engaged in the same math lesson. They had similar demographics and a wide range of students. But there, the resemblance ended. In teacher-centered Classroom A, all was chaos as the teacher struggled to control the class and keep students on task. Kids were drawing on their worksheets, arguing, refusing to work. The teacher was nearly at her wits' end trying to get them focused.

Down the hall in Classroom B, there was plenty of chatter as kids worked in teams of four or five, but the teacher was weaving between teaming groups, quietly redirecting kids if they strayed off task. She gave kids frequent feedback as she addressed each group. She kept her voice low and her demeanor calm. And although the room was messy and a bit noisy, it was never chaotic. I could tell that the lesson was progressing nicely, the students were engaged, and that they were staying on task. As she encountered resistance here or there, I saw that she had devised techniques to address behavior issues as part of her lesson planning.

What is our takeaway from this observation?

When you begin to incorporate teaming structures, you'll want to plan for the kinds of behaviors you're likely to encounter during a lesson. Plan how often and in what way you will intervene when students are rebellious, too rowdy, defiant, or off task. It's important to think about how and when to pick your battles, so you don't disrupt the students' learning.

Techniques for Addressing Issues of Behavior

DEFIANCE

What do I do if I have a defiant student or students?

They may be refusing to do the work, copying others' work, not performing their assigned roles, playing rather than working, straying off task, writing notes, checking phones, etc.

Try these techniques:

- Have a one-on-one conversation quietly with the student, speaking respectfully. Is there an issue they need to chat about? Is the problem with the group dynamic, or the individual student? Try not to take the student out of the team dynamic if possible; if it's necessary, do so only very briefly.

- If a whispered conversation in the student's team isn't appropriate, try a tap on the shoulder and a request that the student take a walk with you. Keep it low-key. See if you can get to the root cause of the defiance without causing major disruptions.

- Students can be taught techniques for self-soothing. Provide students with strategies to help them calm down. They might take a trip to the water fountain, take a deep breath, or use picture cues to process how to deal with stress. (See figure 3.2.)

- Remind the group of their individual roles. Does everyone in the group understand their responsibilities?

- Enlist the team facilitator (see the appendix). Ask if you need to intervene, or if the facilitator can pull the student back into the group work.

Facilitator

Ensures that students participate equally by encouraging quiet students and helping active students to allow others to talk. Asks guiding questions and ensures the discussion stays focused on critical content and task completion.

Figure 3.1: Cards taped to desks can help students remember their roles.

- Gently remind the team of expected norms, using the anchor chart.

- If the situation is escalating, think about reorganizing the team and regrouping with different members.

- Remember: the less commotion a teacher makes, the more likely a defiant student will be to come around.

DEPENDENCE

What do I do if a student relies too much on me as a teacher?

You may have a struggling student who is frightened of failure or of looking stupid. Or you may have a high-achieving student who demands constant reinforcement and attention. These students often ask for your reassurance before they are able to move on with their

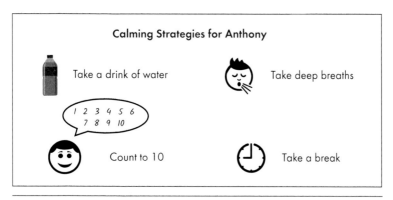

Figure 3.2: In one classroom, the teacher taped these reminders to a student's desk because he was having trouble keeping calm and self-soothing.

assigned task. You may notice that they call you over to answer questions even when their teammates can answer them.

Try these techniques:

- Revisit team norms and expectations for independent work.

- Have team members check their own work against posted success criteria.

- Ask the whole team to look for evidence that the learning target has been met.

- Remind students to use their resources (notes, anchor charts, electronic devices, classmates, books, etc.).

- Remind the student that they can always check their work with their own team, or their team can verify with another team.

- After these steps, verify the learning for the whole team, or clear up misconceptions.

CAN'T FOLLOW ROUTINES

What do I do if I have a student who doesn't follow routines?

They may be talking out of turn, being disrespectful to their teammates, or not contributing based on the expectations of their roles.

Try these techniques:

- Have students tape the class norms to their desks as a constant reminder. This leaves them no excuse for not knowing expectations.

- Gently and respectfully redirect.

- Enlist the help of the facilitator to reinforce routines in a polite manner.

- Create hand symbols for the often-missed routines so that you can signal the student from across the room.

- The next time you start a task, remind students of the most commonly missed routines.

CAN'T SIT STILL

What do I do if I have a student who won't sit still?

We all have students who are all over the classroom. Or students who struggle to concentrate and have a difficult time sitting in one spot listening for too long.

Try these techniques:

- Don't overreact to activity. As long as movement is not disrupting the learning or putting students in danger, activity means engagement. Keep restless students moving, but don't let the learning stop.

- Give the restless student a small task or errand. They can bring something to another teacher's class or be the person who turns off the light.

- Invest in a couple of seating options such as exercise balls or wobbly balance chairs and only allow students to sit in them if they are still learning.

- Let kids own their classroom. Allow students to lie on their stomachs, sit on stools, stand up, move about the classroom, sit on beanbag chairs, etc. As long as students are working, let them choose how and where they group.

- If things begin to get out of hand, suggest that the team move to another place, sit on the carpet, etc.

A Behavioral Specialist Reflects on Strategies for Reducing Misbehavior

Student behavior is a complex and sometimes confounding issue for teachers. When students misbehave, we want to attribute it to something. Is it because they are bored? Are they confused? Is there something going on at home? We wrack our brains trying to figure out not only what to do, but how to do it, and how to prevent it in the future. To get more background information on this very complicated topic, I reached out to behavioral consultant Paul Gavoni, COO of Kaleidoscope Interventions:

> The simplest and quickest strategy for reducing misbehavior is through effective communication. Communication is relatively complex: It can be used to prevent behavior, start behavior, stop behavior, increase behavior(s) (performance), and decrease behavior. Proximity to students, the smallest facial expression, the slightest change in tone of voice, or the tiniest of gestural movements are forms of communication. One of the keys to effectively influencing behavior through communication is to remember it's not just what you say and how you say it.
>
> Relationships are quickly strengthened through positive interactions paired with calm but consistent corrections. One of the keys to correcting misbehavior is by

speaking in a way that conveys to the student, "I care about you and your achievement." Correcting misbehavior in a way that conveys, "Hey, I hate to do this, but I have to, because it will help you in the future" has the amazing effect of strengthening relationships.

Bottom line, teachers who allow misbehavior to occur in their presence are actually inadvertently condoning it. The message silently communicated to the student and others witnessing the misbehavior is that it must be okay to behave this way, because the teacher is allowing it.

Prior to implementing any of the techniques in this chapter, you may want to ask yourself two general questions:

Is it a skill deficit? In other words, does the student know what to do? Teachers often make the mistake of assuming a student knows what to do because they "told" them. But if it's the beginning of the year or perhaps a new routine is being implemented, students may know what to do, but they simply aren't in the habit of doing it. Punishing them in this case is a recipe for disaster. It will surely hurt your relationship with the student and perhaps create more of the misbehavior you are trying to correct.

Is there a motivational deficit? A couple of common issues linked to motivation might be:

Does the student understand the "why"? In other words, how will the activity or lesson help them, and how is it connected to their previous learning?

Is the activity or lesson engaging? If students are not engaged in the lesson, they will certainly find something else to engage themselves in. Strategies for improving engagement include increasing the pace of instruction, asking lots of well-thought-out questions, and providing plenty of feedback to shape incremental improvements in performance.

Desired Outcome for Behavior

We know that teaming is successful when teams are autonomous, when students are taking ownership of learning, and when they are dealing with issues within the team rather than leaning on the teacher unnecessarily for guidance. We want to free ourselves up to trouble-shoot and facilitate learning, not spend all of our time redirecting students. Students in successful teams will demonstrate self-control and self-regulation. They will understand how to respectfully disagree rather than arguing. They will listen to each other's viewpoints. Students should feel responsible to their team. And finally, they should understand that the work they are doing in teams is helping them build skills that will enable them to interact responsibly with others in their future workplaces.

REFLECTION QUESTIONS

Have you ever felt like you're ready to lose your temper in the classroom? You're not alone. But next time, remember that your reaction to misbehavior can make or break your lesson.

- Ask yourself: How can I keep from overreacting and dial down my response to keep the flow of the lesson moving without interrupting the learning?

- How can I plan techniques for specific students I know may have behavior issues?

FURTHER READING

How to Engage Students Who Act Out by Mary Damer

Quick Wins by Paul Gavoni and Manuel Rodriguez

4

Addressing Issues with Academics

When I work with my group I can feel my brain getting stronger! We get to help each other learn and take turns teaching and listening. We know that when we say it, it goes to our brains, and helps us remember.

—Kindergarten student, Jackson, TN

I was not up to the idea of group work. I'd rather know that I'm going to do my work, and if I don't, it's my fault. But actually, group work ended up helping me. Once I realized history isn't my strongest subject and I needed others' input to understand the concepts, working in teams actually helped me out a lot.

—High school student, Columbus, GA

I feel confident when I walk in the room and I know I'm the leader, and I might have to teach people in my group. It feels good to know I'm the one helping others.

—High school student, Des Moines, IA

Overview

Many teachers new to teaming are surprised that students are able to learn autonomously and use complex problem-solving techniques by drawing on resources independently or collaborating with teammates. As teachers, though we don't mean to have low expectations for students, we are not accustomed to letting them solve problems on their own. But we will never know what students are capable of unless we give them a chance. We have often seen students figure out independently or with peers how to use a computer program, or how to navigate through applications they have never seen before. Given the opportunity, they may just need a bit of push or some direction. Instead of relying on direct instruction and overcontrolling the process, we must remember to maintain our growth mindsets by transferring ownership of learning to our students. Work on changing the classroom culture, little by little, so that students understand that failure plays a vital role in the learning process.

For example, Aliyah was a very low-performing third-grade student. She was in a Tier 3 intervention group due to below-level proficiency in reading. She also qualified for the after-school tutoring program, which her parents immediately signed her up for because she needed the help, but even more so because free dinner was provided.

Aliyah was often in a reading group with ESOL students who were new to the country because they were the only students at her academic level. When that didn't seem to meet her needs, Aliyah was put on remediation at the computer station. Other kids were working in teams—socializing, problem solving, interacting with their classmates—and it was oftentimes their favorite part of the school day. Not Aliyah. Aliyah was either with the teacher or alone on the computer, being guided through activities directed by the voice on the screen.

When it came time for lunch, PE, or recess, Aliyah was often left out because she didn't have a peer group. She had no friends because she was rarely able to interact with other students.

For Aliyah, school was tough, and it didn't matter how many times she was pulled out for interventions or provided incentives; she was not achieving, mostly because she had extremely low confidence and was beginning to hate school. School felt like drill and kill, focused on assessments and far too many conversations about data. There was little to no opportunity for her to interact with her peers, so school was never about just being a kid.

What is our takeaway from this story?

When dealing with issues of academics, particularly with students who have been underperforming, it's important to remember not to pull them out of teamwork. Teaming will strengthen their academic and social skills, and it will also have a positive impact on their self-confidence and belief in their ability to do the work and meet learning targets.

Techniques for Addressing Academic Issues

What do I do if a student has low verbal skills (ELL, ESOL, English language) or disabilities?

These students may be unable to keep up with classroom discussion or instruction due to translation issues; unable to contribute to team conversations if content is not easily translatable (using figurative language, idioms, etc.); or lacking confidence in their verbal abilities.

Try these techniques:

- Provide the student with support, but keep the student in the group, not in a separate low-level team. For example, you might provide picture clues to go with words.

Figure 4.1: Posters and visuals help students remember the teaming processes you are putting in place and give them clear expectations.

- Pair the student occasionally (but not always!) with students who speak and understand the same language.

- Utilize school support such as paraprofessionals, speech therapists, English language facilitators, or coteachers to help the student *within* the group, not separately.

- Ask the facilitator to specifically reword questions or statements for the student.

- Provide time for students to think or draw before they share their answers with their peers to give the students time to come up with the right words.

LOW ABILITY

What do I do if I have a student who is unable to do the work?

The student may be below grade level in reading and/or math

proficiency. These students often have low confidence when it comes to working in teams because they don't believe they can contribute with others.

Try these techniques:

- Put students in mixed-ability groups with mixed interests, and provide structure for student teams to support and coach each other.

- Provide specific supports to the students to allow them to participate in the conversation even if they cannot do all of the work independently (highlight the key sections of the reading, provide multiplication charts).

- Check in with students while they are working with their team. Give them a brief pep talk. Individualize support, but don't single students out unnecessarily.

- Notice what academic support the student needs and provide it in general statements to the team or class.

- If necessary, pull students aside for brief reteach or mini-lessons, but get them back into the group as soon as possible to practice with their team.

- Check in with students' teammates or facilitators. Ask the team to try to explain the problem or concept to the student rather than you reteaching.

- If the team's learning is getting interrupted or losing velocity, pull the student out for a brief one-on-one. It's important that a struggling student not feel like an impediment to the team.

What do I do if I have a whole team that is unable to do the work?

We are accountable for our students. When the task is beyond the academic level of the team, we can't let them struggle to the point where no learning is occurring. If the team is at a standstill, it's our job to know when to intervene or clear up misconceptions. We can't expect the heavy lift to come from the team if learning has stalled or if the struggle is no longer productive.

Try these techniques:

- Consider a small reteach lesson to that individual team. You may want to spend a little extra time with them to get them started.

- Switch up the team members to see if another student may be able to help the team.

- Have the facilitator rotate to support other teams, then bring them back to the original team.

HIGH-PERFORMING RESISTERS

What do I do if I have high-performing students who resent or complain about low-performing students? Or high-performing students who resist working in teams?

They may be above average and may not want to work in teams because they fear being held back or slowed down by team members.

When students are advanced and don't believe that their group is at the same level, they may hesitate about participating in teamwork. In most cases, however, these students end up realizing that they will learn so much from the perspectives of their peers. They will also begin to deepen their knowledge by mentoring less advanced students.

Try these techniques:

- Create structures that require all students to share their thinking so that the high-performing student isn't giving the answer to the other students.

- Use gems. Students are each given a few gems (or tokens) for group conversations. Students make a fixed number of contributions: They put a gem in the center of the table each time they contribute, and also learn to listen when they have used up all their gems. Students don't always understand that being an *active listener* is an important part of contributing to the team.

- If the high achiever is opting not to share their answer, let them go last and remind them that all team members need to contribute.

- Ask students to reflect on their contribution to the team to highlight the need for all students to participate.

- Redirect the student's energy away from complaints by making the high-performing student the team facilitator. This adds a level of responsibility that high performers tend to love.

- Give your high performers a one-on-one pep talk. Tell them, "You will be my team lead." Challenge them to find ways to help their team members without directly providing answers. Challenge them to develop teaming strategies without relying on you.

- Praise progress and wins.

- Offer new challenges with enrichment activities.

Figure 4.2: This poster helps high-achieving students who work fast know what to do when they finish early, setting academic expectations.

FEAR OF FAILURE

What do I do if I have a student who is afraid to fail?

Students may be striving for perfection. High-achieving students often believe that failure is not an option. Low-achieving students may feel battered by earlier failures and become unwilling to even try.

Try these techniques:

- Pair students up with those they already know and trust (in other words, hand select the groups until students are ready to move to randomized teams).

- Provide resources to allow students choice in how they learn best to build confidence.

- ▸ Use a variety of texts, whiteboards, math manipulatives, and audio and visual aids
- Celebrate small successes every day:
  - ▸ Ask kids to write sticky notes celebrating each other's successes, and post them on the wall.
  - ▸ Print classroom motivational signs that encourage perseverance. Be sure that everyone understands that the struggle is an important part of learning.

Some examples we've seen in classrooms:
"Stuck? We're glad you're here."
"A person who never made a mistake never tried anything new."
"I can accept failure ... I can't accept not trying"

  - ▸ Display student work.
  - ▸ Write personal notes, make positive phone calls home, use class-wide incentives.
  - ▸ Showcase wall or bulletin board displays to spotlight students.
  - ▸ Institute Student of the Week (or Month). Be sure to recognize character and effort, not just academics.
  - ▸ Emphasize the concepts of productive struggle and growth mindset.
  - ▸ Offer feedback that is not grade-related. (For example, two stars and a wish, a glow and a grow, are ways to highlight the positives in a students' work while also giving them support on what they need to work on.)

Figure 4.3: Motivational posters help students know that failure is an important part of learning and striving.

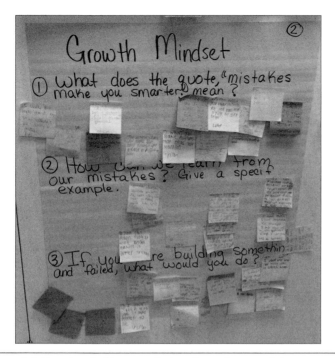

Figure 4.4: Use visual aids to remind students that practicing a growth mindset is nonnegotiable.

Desired Outcome for Academic Teaming

When a team is working together effectively, responsibility for completing problems, assignments, and projects is shared equally. The whole team understands that learning is a collaborative project, and that the team is a safe place to explore ideas, make mistakes, experiment, take risks, and learn together. The team closely resembles real teams in the work world. Team members support one another and allow everyone a chance to contribute. Team members know when to step in and help, but they also know not to take over or oversupport.

REFLECTION QUESTIONS

- How can I stop myself from stepping in when I don't need to?

- How do I let kids teach me and each other?

- What support, in terms of access to resources, can I provide teams so that they have the information and tools they need at their fingertips?

FURTHER READING

Learning to Dream with Your Eyes Wide Open by Melanie D. Geddes

Connecting with Students' Will to Succeed: The Power of Connation by Cheryl R. Gholar and Ernestine G. Riggs

Do You Know Enough About Me to Teach Me? A Student's Perspective by Stephen G. Peters

5

Addressing Issues with Motivation

The teacher doesn't immediately tell us the answer. Giving us the answers doesn't help us learn. Even though it's tough, she gets us to think deeper. We actually do know the answer, we just need to be pushed to get there.

—Tenth-grade student, Ridgely, MD

Overview

Motivational issues are often closely related to academic or behavioral issues. For example, some students' low motivation may be the result of a lack of self-esteem, distracting problems at home, and low skills. While we have addressed each of these issues separately, they often occur together and reinforce each other. In this chapter we will address issues of student self-esteem, challenges at home that affect classroom motivation, and boredom with content.

Melanie Siegel, a fourth-grade teacher in Boca Raton, Florida, told us the following story about a student:

> Mikayla was a student in my class who was frequently discouraged whenever independent work was required of her. She was constantly being pulled for small group instruction, and she often didn't produce much during independent work before or after group. She didn't have a positive attitude toward schoolwork because, for years, she had been constantly behind.

> When Mikayla was introduced to teamwork using success criteria, she felt the positive energy from her peers, who helped [her] feel successful, and that she had good ideas to contribute.
>
> Mikayla felt more positive at school because her team members encouraged her to do her best and helped her see she could use success criteria to measure her progress. Mikayla grew especially in writing: She went from scoring a 1 in each area to scoring an overall score of 6 on the Florida State Assessment, which was a huge improvement.

What is our takeaway from Mikayla's story?

If students are not able to do the work because they have fallen so far behind, they begin to feel alienated. They don't like to come to school, they don't feel like they belong in the community, and because they are so often pulled out for independent work, they miss out on critical peer interaction. Mikayla was a compliant child; she wasn't misbehaving. But she was frustrated and just plain sad. We can all see that if a child already feels this way in fourth grade, it's only going to get harder as time goes on. The child is in danger of hating school.

This teacher wasn't sure how to pair Mikayla with others because she didn't realize that Mikayla's peers would teach her and strengthen her confidence. She strategically paired high and low performers on a team, and Mikayla began to blossom.

Techniques for Addressing Motivation Issues

SELF-ESTEEM ISSUES

What do I do if a student is not motivated to learn due to low self-esteem or prior negative learning experiences?

Try these techniques:

- Scaffold or chunk the learning. Break the task into smaller pieces so that the student is able to experience small successes.

- Give more frequent feedback to keep the student moving forward. Be sure that peers are offering feedback that helps the student move forward.

- Pair the student with a student who is academically accomplished and who has a calm demeanor. That student can coach without getting frustrated or upset, and acting as peer-teacher will also help the high learner.

- Remember to celebrate small successes. Small achievements build confidence.

- Encourage the student to keep track of their progress in planners, using stickers or telling you during formal or informal chats.

- Call the student's home with positive news and praise.

- Organize groups with mixed abilities so that students are able to lean on each other's strengths.

- Don't take away routines, privileges, or stations that other students are allowed to participate in, such as recess, computer time, work stations/centers, and so on. Peer interaction is important.

HOME ISSUES

What do I do if I have a student who is distracted by life issues or home issues?

Try these techniques:

- Endeavor to make the classroom a *home away from home*.

    ‣ The classroom should be a place where students are equal and respected. Provide a variety of books and visual aids celebrating different cultures, recognizing diversity.

▸ Make the atmosphere free of stress. Plants, sunlight, displays of student work, comfortable seating options, area rugs and curtains, lamps for corner reading areas, and music when appropriate can all have a soothing effect.

▸ Ensure that supplies are abundant.

■ Make an effort to be welcoming and kind to every student. Stand at the door and welcome students every day.

■ Make sure that every day is a fresh start. Don't hold over behavior issues from previous classes.

■ Keep nutritious snacks in the classroom for kids who might be hungry.

BOREDOM WITH CONTENT

What do I do if I have a student who is bored with the content?

Try these techniques:

■ Consider the diverse backgrounds in your classroom, the mix of genders, and current trends. Is there a way to engage students by drawing on their interests?

■ Use friendly controversy about current events that students can relate to or find highly interesting when planning activities.

■ Change up classroom activities to allow students to get up and move around the classroom. Try gallery walks; vote with your feet; changing up the groups; using whiteboards, artwork, or audio/visual; or giving them more active ways to use their mobile devices.

■ If time permits, allow students to explore the content further: for example, internet research on related topics, books dealing with a similar subject, magazine articles, interviews, etc.

- Ensure that your routines are consistent, but that activities are frequently changing. Students can write, draw, act, play games, etc.

- Plan for brain breaks or team-building activities.

- Plan for student choice in seating arrangements.

- Plan for student choice in which assignments to tackle.

- Mix student strengths and interests when composing teams.

- Plan for hands-on, project-based learning.

- Advanced: Let students choose their own groups—but this should be an earned privilege. For example, at the end of a unit, students may want to organize themselves based on interests, reading materials, etc.

What do I do if I have a student who is not motivated to learn due to self-esteem issues or negative learning experiences? Or if I have a student who is overwhelmed by the content?

Try these techniques:

- Scaffold or chunk the learning by breaking the task into smaller pieces.

- Give more frequent feedback (from both teachers and peers) to keep the student moving forward.

- Pair with another student who is academically high-achieving, has a calm demeanor, and can coach without getting frustrated or upset.

- Celebrate small successes to keep the team going.

- Keep track of progress in planners (stickers, formal or informal chats).

- Positive phone calls home.

- Create teams with mixed abilities so that students lean on each other's strengths.

- Don't use teaming as a reward. Don't take away student work time at centers, student work time within teams, or recess. Peer interaction is important.

Desired Outcome for Students Experiencing Motivation Issues

We want our students to come to school knowing each day is a safe, fresh start, a new opportunity to be successful. Kids are just like adults; sometimes they have off days, but our job is to keep them motivated. Things happen before they get to school—we don't necessarily need to know all the details, but we do need to think of different ways to pique their interest, to be flexible, and to keep some tricks in our toolbox when they seem to lack motivation. Every day is different. This is what we love about teaching. Ask yourself, are you bored as you teach and plan the lesson? If so, chances are the students are going to be, too. When you are excited, your enthusiasm is reflected in your teaching and in your students' engagement.

REFLECTION QUESTIONS

- How can I make sure *all* students are included?
- What can I do to build relationships with my students to better understand their backgrounds?
- How can I remind myself to incorporate a variety of activities to keep students engaged?

FURTHER READING

20 Strategies for STEM Instruction by William N. Bender

Engaging the Rewired Brain by David A. Sousa

6

Addressing Issues of Personality

Working in a Title 1 inner-city school is hard enough. Teaching kindergarten in inner-city schools while trying to implement group work seemed next to impossible. I wondered how it would be possible for students coming from such diverse backgrounds to be able to work together. Group work, however, has been one of the key driving factors in my students' success. They learn everything, from social skills to time management to teamwork, all of which are necessary life skills for success outside the classroom. Classroom time becomes so much more than teaching to a test, which for a teacher is a breath of fresh air.

—Melissa Smith, kindergarten teacher, Jackson, TN

Overview

Personality issues intersect with behavior issues, discussed in chapter 2, in ways that we can't always isolate: personality drives behavior, and behavior often reflects personality. Further, students come to us from all different walks of life, and their personality is often influenced by their background.

For example, if a student is part of a family where all decisions are made by parents, the student may have a difficult time problem solving without the direct support of a teacher. Students who are more reserved and depend on their parents may struggle with being the facilitator of a team. They may never have been in charge before, so they may have to be taught how to lead. As teachers, we need to build their confidence and create a positive classroom culture that encourages productive struggle, where all students thrive in a student-centered learning environment.

In this chapter we address issues with communication, social skills, timidity, and personality conflicts in teams.

Students Reflect on Teaming

"If I don't get a problem right I feel defeated; that's just my personality. I'm not easygoing, and I want to get things done. But after we implemented teams, I felt better about concepts I didn't understand. I felt good with the idea, and at the end of the day I didn't feel defeated at all."

—High school student, Des Moines, IA

"Working in teams makes you grow as a person, because if there is someone in your group you don't get along with, your teacher is not going to care. You have to get over it because when you are out in the real world you won't be able to choose who you have to work with."

—High school student, Ridgely, MD

What is our takeaway from these students' reflections?

One of the students we quote above was a high achiever, but her discomfort with failure was a sign that she needed to build resilience and a growth mindset, and to cultivate the kind of solid self-esteem that could transcend occasional disappointments.

We meet students like this every day. At one top-ranked magnet high school, students were so accustomed to doing their own individual work, and to having "control" of their work, that they were often reluctant to collaborate in teams or to act as team facilitators. We heard students say, again and again, that they needed validation from their teachers to know that they were "right" or were performing well. Surprisingly, these high performers lacked confidence. They had trouble trusting both their own judgment and the judgments of their peers. In many cases these students were anxious perfectionists who held rigid ideas about schooling, the learning process, and the meaning of success. Getting them to team required changing some deeply held habits. They had to begin to *own* their learning in a way that was not dependent on teacher validation, and to own the learning of their teams.

Over time, these students did learn to collaborate. They came to appreciate the value of team effort: they found meaning in contributing to a larger whole, sought out the views of others, and understood how learning about and discussing those views deepened their own learning. Teaming allowed students to practice and refine social and emotional skills, to learn to respectfully agree or disagree, to examine their assumptions, and to understand that there is often more than one right answer. All these skills are required in the twenty-first-century workplace. They are also skills even *adults* can struggle to master!

Techniques for Addressing Issues of Personality

COMMUNICATION

What do I do if I have a student who is overly assertive, or who is monopolizing the conversation?

Try these techniques:

- Ensure that you have clear team roles. If a facilitator or student in another role is dominating conversations, change up roles as necessary to shift responsibilities.

- Ensure that you have created an environment of high expectations for all students. How do students know that they are expected to contribute, or make a space for others to do so?

- Post norms and expectations for group communication. (See appendix for other examples.)

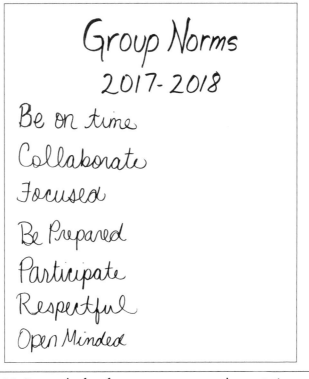

Figure 6.1: Post and refer often to team norms and expectations.

- Use a talking stick. Students speak only when they are holding the stick.
- Use gems to encourage contributions. (See page 46 for an explanation of gems.)
- Give students anchor charts or posted norms to refer to.

What do I do if I have a student who lacks communication and/ or social skills?

As we touched on above, these are skills we all (even as adults) struggle to master, so helping students build communication and social skills early will benefit them over a lifetime.

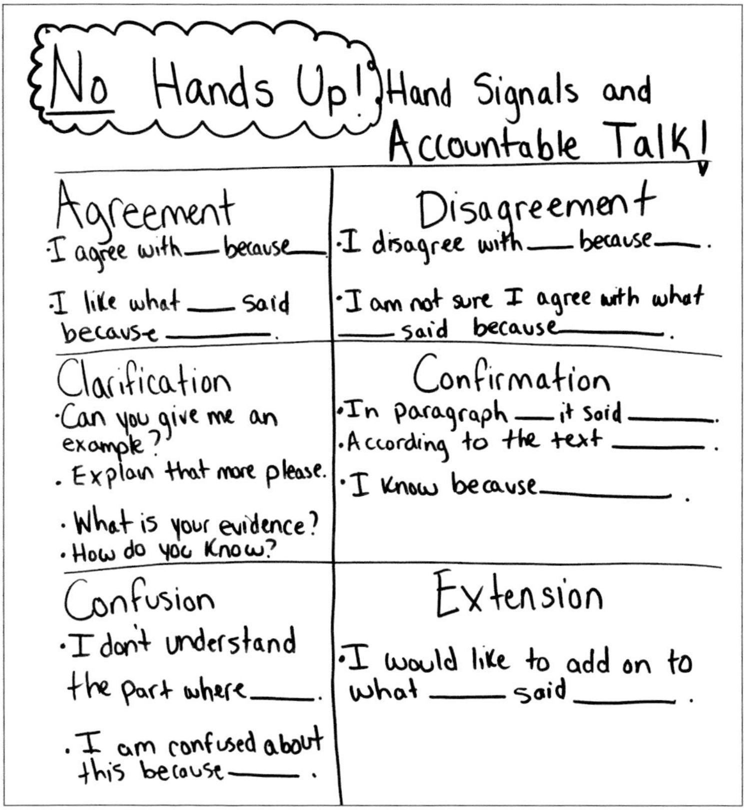

Figure 6.2: Post norms for accountable talk to ensure that all students contribute to the team effort and conversation.

Try these techniques:

- Give students feedback conversation stems for agreeing, disagreeing, and requesting clarification.

- Provide visual aids for students working in teams. These may be reminders about who talks first, and for how long. It's important to include visuals for our ELL students and nonreaders.

- "Hands off/ears out/mouth off." A posted visual reminder tells students that they need to control their actions and speech, and be active listeners. The visual helps remind students not to take over the conversation, interrupt learning, or to do the work for others.

■ Practice using active listening skills with students before they begin teamwork and continue to practice throughout.

■ Understand that not all students arrive at school with the same communication skills. Families may have wildly different communication strategies. Model the communication you want to see, continue to remind students of expectations, and be sure to praise when they are communicating well.

■ Practice mock disagreements in class to teach students to politely disagree. Students love to role-play, and this strategy gives them the chance to see expected behavior with examples and nonexamples.

■ Teach students to respond instead of react. Children who come from difficult environments may not find this a natural strategy. But you can help them practice with modeling, reminders, praise, and role-playing.

■ Teach students the meaning of constructive criticism. Students should practice giving criticism without being rude or hurting others' feelings. They should also practice receiving constructive criticism without taking it personally. Hearing criticism about our work or ideas can be difficult even for adults, but starting these conversations early, with continuous modeling in the classroom, will teach students to accept and give feedback effectively.

■ Use team-building activities to build self-esteem and confidence.

Give Them a Brain Break

Students occasionally need a brain break. Have students do team-building activities to get them more comfortable with their classmates. In one class, students wrote positive characteristics about their friends on paper plates taped to their backs. After the activity was finished, students had a combination of positive words to describe themselves! Students who completed this activity referred to their paper plates when they felt down or experienced low self-esteem. Remember: students may not get compliments at home. It's part of our job as teachers to lift them up and make them feel important.

Figure 6.3: Team-building activities like this one, where students write down positive qualities about each other, help build their confidence and self-esteem.

QUIET OR TIMID STUDENTS

What do I do if I have a student who is too quiet or timid to participate fully?

We often attribute shyness to low self-esteem. But low self-esteem isn't always the root cause of shyness. Quiet students may just be introverted, or they may not have had much practice speaking in front of large groups, or they may even come from a home where they don't get many opportunities to talk. They also may not have had sufficient opportunities to speak aloud in previous grades or in other classrooms. Excellent oral communication is highly prized in the workplace. We can't allow shy kids to fall through the cracks by failing to help them build communication skills.

Try these techniques:

- Manage response rates with techniques like no hands up, random calling, or response boards to ensure that all students have opportunities to respond verbally and visually.

- Create a strong team and classroom culture to build cohesion and show inclusiveness for all students: handshakes, team names, etc.

- Have students practice talking in front of partners or smaller groups, then build to talking within teams or in front of the class as a whole.

- Don't publicly urge students to talk when they are nervous. Move in and speak to them one-on-one.

- Give students options for responding—not all communication must be verbal (hand signals, whiteboards, electronic communication, etc.).

"I have a student who in years past would not speak at all. She literally would crouch in the corner. She didn't respond positively to any adults in the building. And now, after we have been doing teaming, I've noticed a huge change. She's laughing and giggling. I can see that working in teams and with partners instead of interacting with only the adults has helped her. To observe her feeling positive about herself with her team is a pretty cool thing."

—Laura Royer, fifth-grade teacher, Preston, MD

What do I do if I have students who are timid about speaking up in diverse groups?

Try these techniques:

- Make sure to mix genders and cultures in groups so that students can practice speaking up.

- Promote equality in the classroom. Consciously work

against stereotypes or bias around gender, race, sexual orientation, or culture.

- Use a randomizer or popsicle sticks to call on students to avoid preconceived expectations.

- Distribute roles equitably.

- Learn about students' interests, and encourage nonstereotyped hobbies, careers, and interests.

- Provide a rich library of diverse books celebrating all cultures.

- Provide real-life examples of opportunities for all genders and cultures.

PERSONALITY CONFLICTS

What do I do if I have students who are not getting along?

Not every student is going to get along perfectly with every other student. They may have personal issues outside the classroom that interfere with smooth teaming, or they may simply rub each other the wrong way. But that doesn't mean they can't work together.

Try these techniques:

- Directly teach conflict-resolution skills, including role-playing.

- Resist the urge to step in immediately. It's okay to let students struggle with personality conflicts. Give them a chance to figure it out, and encourage team members to productively engage in the issue to resolve it.

- When it's time to intervene, suggest that the students having a conflict take a break, take a walk, get a drink, or do something else to ease the tension.

- Offer a temporary solution. Journal writing, meditating, joining a different team, and working for a few minutes independently are possibilities. But remember, the goal is to get the students back to their original team.

- If learning is being significantly interrupted, switch up the teams.

Desired Outcome for Students Experiencing Personality Issues

Students should understand that in the real world, working teams will not always be a perfect mix of personalities, skill levels, and character traits. We all will have to work with peers who are occasionally overly assertive, who don't contribute as much as we would hope, or who push our buttons. But knowing how to deal with situations where conflicts arise will help our students in school and life. As I've noted above, as adults, we are still working on these skills nearly every day.

REFLECTION QUESTIONS

- How can I help students understand that working together in a team is not necessarily about liking everyone they work with, but rather about respecting each other and collaborating in an effective way? That these are life skills that will help them in their careers and future grades?

- What can I do to remind myself to support teams without "fixing" the problems if and when they occur?

FURTHER READING

Productive Group Work by Nancy Frey, Douglas Fisher, and Sandi Everlove

Working with Students: Discipline Strategies for the Classroom by Ruby Payne

Final Thought

"Changing our classrooms to reflect the world of today and tomorrow certainly requires an investment of effort. But once students become engaged in the real-world complex tasks and are eager to reach learning targets for themselves and their teams, it will pay off for the rest of our teaching careers. The good news is that students are coming to us prewired for this transformed new economy classroom learning environment. We just have to tap into it."

—Michael Toth, *Who Moved My Standards?*
Joyful Teaching in an Age of Change

Now you're on your way to teaming. Remember to keep this guide handy and refer to it as often as you need. Like all teachers who implement teaming, you will struggle at first, but don't worry. The object is not to be perfect right away. As we have heard from so many teachers, teaming with your students in the classroom is life changing. Good luck!

Appendix:
Templates for Teaming

Ask a Question or Give a Suggestion That Will Help Your Partner

Feedback Question Stems

Have you tried ...?

Did you think about ...?

I wonder if ...?

Can you tell me more about...?

Why did you choose to...?

Revise Your Work

Reflection Questions

What could I do differently next time?

How can I use this in the future?

How confident am I that I can do this by myself?

Is there a better strategy than the one I used?

Working with a Partner

Working with a Partner

Partner A: Share your thinking
Partner B: Make eye contact and listen for understanding

Partner B: Share your thinking
Partner A: Make eye contact and listen for understanding

A & B: Compare how your thinking is the same and different
- We agree that ...
- We disagree that ...

Working with a Partner

Partner A: Share your thinking
Partner B: Make eye contact and listen for understanding

Partner B: Share your thinking
Partner A: Make eye contact and listen for understanding

A & B: Compare how your thinking is the same and different
- We agree that ...
- We disagree that ...

Working with a Partner

Partner A: Share your thinking
Partner B: Make eye contact and listen for understanding

Partner B: Share your thinking
Partner A: Make eye contact and listen for understanding

A & B: Compare how your thinking is the same and different
- We agree that ...
- We disagree that ...

Working with a Partner

Partner A: Share your thinking
Partner B: Make eye contact and listen for understanding

Partner B: Share your thinking
Partner A: Make eye contact and listen for understanding

A & B: Compare how your thinking is the same and different
- We agree that ...
- We disagree that ...

Team Talk	**Team Talk**

Question Prompts:

Can you explain?

Which part of the success criteria does that meet?

What should we do next?

Why do you think that?

Can you support your opinion?

Can you give me an example from the text?

Where can I find that in the text?

Is there another way we can solve this?

What strategy should we use?

Have we met the Success Criteria yet? Why or why not?

Question Prompts:

Can you explain?

Which part of the success criteria does that meet?

What should we do next?

Why do you think that?

Can you support your opinion?

Can you give me an example from the text?

Where can I find that in the text?

Is there another way we can solve this?

What strategy should we use?

Have we met the Success Criteria yet? Why or why not?

Conflict Resolution Protocol

Conflict	Resolution The facilitator should lead this process.
If an argument between group members happens...	• Take a break for a few moments. • Let the members share their thoughts calmly without interruptions. • Brainstorm solutions to resolve the conflict and get back on track.
Misunderstanding or miscommunication?	• Restate what you were trying to say. • Hear each other's views/sides out before responding.
A group member gets upset and stops working.	• Have the student give an explanation for why they're upset. • Be clear and truthful about what is bothering you and what you need. • Try to meet the needs of the student. • Refocus and get back on task.

Facilitator

Get the conversation started quickly.

Ask all teammates to share their ideas/questions.

Encourage everyone to contribute.

Learning Monitor

Help all teammates understand the success criteria at the beginning.

Remind teammates to use success criteria as they work.

Ask questions to see if the completed work meets the success criteria.

Partner Conversations	
Looks like	Sounds like
2 students	On task
Turn to one another	Both partners speak
Speaker is speaking	I agree because
Listener is listening	I disagree because
	I want to add on to what you said

Team Norms Examples

EXAMPLE 1

1. Listen to everyone's ideas.
2. Take turns speaking so everyone has a chance.
3. No one is done until everyone is done.
4. Remember to follow your group role.
5. Consider new ideas.

EXAMPLE 2

1. Everyone is respectful.
2. Stay on task.
3. If you have a question, don't be afraid to ask.
4. Everyone should participate.
5. Share any successes.

Inspirational/Motivational Posters

Every time
That I feel myself
about to sink...

I swim
just a little bit
HARDER.

> The one that is
> doing the Talking is
> the one that is
> doing the Learning.

Desk Reminders

1

Questions to Push Your Thinking	Sharing Feedback	Revising Thinking and Reflection
• Can you explain your thinking? • Does anyone agree/disagree/have more to add? • Why do you disagree? • Why do you think that? • Can you prove it? • What is your evidence? • Do you have anything that is the same/different?	• Have you tried ...? • Did you think about ...? • I agree/disagree because ... • What would happen if ...? • I like the way you ... • Can you tell me more about ...? • Why did you ...? • Is there another way that you can ...?	• Have I met the success criteria? • How confident am I that I can do this by myself? • What should I do better? • How can I use this in the future? • What was important about this? • How can I make this better? • How strong is my evidence?

Training for Teaming

IGNITE CORE INSTRUCTION

Ignite Core Instruction is designed to help students increase their active cognitive engagement and critical thinking skills, which they need to attain the rigor of the new academic standards and skills necessary to thrive in the new economy. To learn more, visit https://www.learningsciences.com/ignite/.

QUICK REFERENCE GUIDES

How to Engage Students Who Act Out by Mary Damer: https://www.learningsciences.com/how-to-engage-students-who-act-out-quick-reference-guide

SOAR Quick Reference Guide by Michael D. Toth: https://www.learningsciences.com/soar-quick-reference-guide

Engaging the Rewired Brain by David A. Sousa: https://www.learningsciences.com/engaging-the-rewired-brain-qrg

BOOKS

Who Moved My Standards? Joyful Teaching in an Age of Change by Michael D. Toth: https://www.learningsciences.com/books/who-moved-my-standards-joyful-teaching-in-an-age-of-change

Engaging the Rewired Brain by David A. Sousa: https://www.learningsciences.com/books/engaging-the-rewired-brain

20 Strategies for Increasing Student Engagement by William N. Bender: https://www.learningsciences.com/books/20-strategies-for-increasing-student-engagement

20 Strategies for Working with Challenging Students by William N. Bender: https://www.learningsciences.com/books/20-disciplinary-strategies-for-working-with-challenging-students

References

Dujon, A. M. (2018). *The gritty truth of school transformation: Eight phases of growth to instructional rigor.* West Palm Beach, FL: Learning Sciences International.

Dweck, C. (n.d.). What is mindset. Retrieved from http://mindsetonline.com/whatisit/about/

Gaulden, J., & Gottlieb, A. (2017). *The age of agility.* Retrieved from http://theageofagility.org

Grit [Def. 4]. (n.d.). In *Merriam-Webster Online.* Retrieved March 15, 2018, from https://www.merriam-webster.com/dictionary/grit

Johnson, D. W., & Johnson, R. T. (1994). *Learning together and alone: Cooperative, competitive, and individualistic learning* (4th ed.). Boston, MA: Allyn & Bacon.

Meister, J. (2012, August 14). The future of work: Job hopping is the 'new normal' for millennials. *Forbes.* Retrieved from https://www.forbes.com/sites/jeannemeister/2012/08/14/the-future-of-work-job-hopping-is-the-new-normal-for-millennials/#5cd6cd0013b8

NACE Center. (2016). Job outlook 2016: The attributes employers want to see on new college graduates' resumes. Retrieved from http://www.naceweb.org/career-development/trends-and-predictions/job-outlook-2016-attributes-employers-want-to-see-on-new-college-graduates-resumes/

Toth, M. D. (2016). *Who moved my standards? Joyful teaching in an age of change: A SOAR-ing tale.* West Palm Beach, FL: Learning Sciences International.

World Economic Forum. (2018, January 24). *Jack Ma: "Everything we teach should be different from machines."* [Video file]. Retrieved from https://www.youtube.com/watch?v=pa2EMaGPZKc

World Economic Forum. (2018, January 24). *Jack Ma: "If we do not change the way we teach, thirty years later we will be in trouble."* [Video file]. Retrieved from https://www.youtube.com/watch?v=pQCF3PtAaSg

Notes

Notes

Notes